YORKSHIRE & HUMBERSIDE TRACTION

Gordon Edgar

AMBERLEY

Front cover: Class 55 Deltic No. 55004 *Queen's Own Highlander* prepares to depart from York, heading the 22.30 King's Cross–Edinburgh service on 26 July 1980.

Back cover: 37708, bearing the Railfreight Petroleum sector decals, heads the 6E39 Mostyn–Hull acetic acid tanks through Castleford on 23 July 1997.

First published 2015

Amberley Publishing
The Hill, Stroud
Gloucestershire, GL5 4EP

www.amberley-books.com

Copyright © Gordon Edgar, 2015

The right of Gordon Edgar to be identified as the Author of this work has been asserted in accordance with the Copyrights, Designs and Patents Act 1988.

ISBN 978 1 4456 4317 5 (print)
ISBN 978 1 4456 4333 5 (ebook)

British Library Cataloguing in Publication Data.
A catalogue record for this book is available from the British Library.

Typesetting by Amberley Publishing.
Printed in the UK.

Introduction

The historic county of Yorkshire, often affectionately referred to as 'God's own country', is the largest county in England and is widely considered to be among the greenest, due to the vast stretches of unspoiled countryside in the Yorkshire Dales and North York Moors and to the open aspect of some of the major cities, as well as the level of rainfall on the moorland regions and Pennine range, of course! The landscape is picturesque and varied, from the Pennines, forming the western boundary of the county, through the Yorkshire Dales, the flatlands of the vales of York and Pickering across to the North Yorkshire Moors, with its delightful coastline and popular tourist seaside destinations of Whitby and Scarborough. Humberside, its name now only used as a geographic term, was a non-metropolitan and ceremonial county in northern England from April 1974 until April 1996. The Humberside region has, and continues to offer, much of interest to the rail enthusiast, with its busy ports of Immingham, Grimsby, Hull and Goole, the vast steelworks complex at Scunthorpe and the resultant supporting rail services that ply the routes through the flatlands bordering the Humber estuary.

A book of this size cannot adequately cover every single aspect of motive power or multiple unit that has historically operated or has been noted in the region, but within these pages an emphasis has been placed on the past rather than the present, apart from special events or recent unusual workings. Resultantly, very few images featuring the ubiquitous General Motors Class 66 are to be found here. An attempt has been made to feature geographically as much of this vast region as possible, outlined in the map below showing the routes in around 1982 just after the much lamented Woodhead route had closed. Images are mainly in colour, although a number of monochrome examples have been included where it is deemed appropriate. The region has boasted many fine photographic vantage points and station opportunities over the years and in this book the surface has not even been scratched when one considers the full potential once available

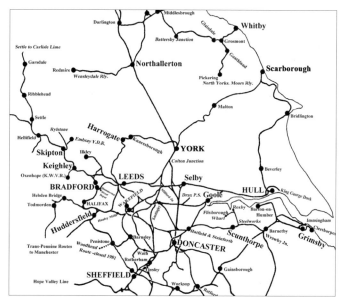

to the photographer. However, an attempt has been made at providing a balanced overview of the traction once synonymous with the region.

British Railways chose West Yorkshire, with its mills and terraced houses of soot-blackened millstone grit, as the region in which to introduce its first production diesel railcars, so it is only right that examples of the types of unit employed over the last half-century are represented in this work. In fact the first DMU operation on BR was introduced in West Yorkshire between Bradford Exchange, Leeds Central and Harrogate in April 1954.

The busy railway centres of York, Doncaster and Leeds have understandably always been a magnet for the enthusiast, particularly during the final years of operation of the iconic Deltic Class 55 and before electrification of the East Coast Main Line. In fact from the first days, when the pilot scheme main-line diesels made an appearance, through to the present day, there have been just a handful of classes in the range of Type 1 to Type 5/classes 01 to 70 that would not have not been seen in or around the region at some stage or other, including those passing through works at Doncaster or those working inter-regional passenger or freight diagrams and special charter trains.

After years of decline from the mid-1970s to the 1990s as diesel and electric multiple units increased in number and the fleet of locomotives reduced dramatically, the railways since privatisation have seen an amazing increase in freight traffic and passenger numbers. While there has been a standardisation of locomotive classes, the liveries of the various train and freight operating companies' locomotives and rolling stock have ensured a continued interest in the contemporary railway scene. To the delight of enthusiasts, some classic diesel locomotive classes, once thought to have been lost from the main line for good, have recently been revived, an exciting development brought about by tighter EU regulations on exhaust emissions for new-build locomotives. The classic examples, possessing the 'grandfather rights' to operate

A scene that epitomises the early years of DMU travel in Yorkshire: a Metropolitan-Cammell three-car unit in dark Brunswick green livery, with unit E50278 trailing, stands in platform 1B at Huddersfield, forming a service to Wakefield Kirkgate on a misty winter's day in the 'pre-whisker' era of the late 1950s, possibly shortly after its delivery in 1957. (Author's Collection)

on the national network regardless of their environmental friendliness, are suddenly in great demand for refurbishment, so who knows what the future holds!

The purpose of this work is to provide the reader with a general overview of the rich tapestry of traction and workings found in the region during the period from the demise of steam traction through to the present day, but with an emphasis on 'classic traction'. Pictures can often tell a thousand words, and the accompanying captions attempt to include as much relevant background information as possible, balanced with the image size constraints possible in a book of this size.

If this work, spanning the half-century or more of 'modern traction' in the region, evokes some treasured memories of the past for the reader I will be delighted. It has been most enjoyable assembling this collection of images, and indeed I have derived much pleasure from living and working in and travelling throughout the region during some of the period covered here. In conclusion, I am indebted to the support that Charlie Cross, Adrian Freeman and Graham Roose have freely given me, and also to John Chalcroft of Railphotoprints for providing some of the more elusive images of the past which I was unable to provide from my own collection; those relevant images are duly credited and, unless otherwise stated, the remaining images were taken by myself.

Gordon Edgar
September 2014

The Birmingham Railway Carriage & Wagon Co. (BRCW) Type 2s (classes 26 and 27) are more generally associated with Scotland, but in their early years the later batch from D5370 to D5415 was to be found in England. A visit to BR Doncaster works on 27 July 1959 found newly delivered D5335 and D5336 (later Class 26 26035 and 26036 respectively) flanking Brush Type 2 D5541 (later 31123), itself brand new from Brush's Falcon works in Loughborough. (www.railphotoprints.co.uk)

Initially a small batch (D5370–D5378) of what was to become Class 27 was allocated to Thornaby (51L), and during the early 1960s made frequent forays into Yorkshire. The BRCW 1,250 hp Type 2s D5370 and D5371 (later 27024 and 27025), working in tandem, were photographed in 1964 heading sheeted mineral wagons north through York station. (Author's Collection)

BR 'Modernisation Plan' – The Early Years

D92, seen here at Leeds Holbeck (55A) in June 1966, was a regular performer on Anglo-Scottish services via the Midland Route at this time. Delivered new in March 1961 from BR Crewe works to Derby depot, it was eventually renumbered 45138 under the TOPS scheme. Withdrawn in March 1987, it was cut up at MC Metals, Glasgow, during April 1994 after long-term storage at March depot. (Charlie Cross)

Brush Type 4 D1993, in the company of D1815 and D1994 at Leeds Holbeck motive power depot in July 1966. Still very much a steam depot then, it is easy to see why, with D1993 barely four months old, diesel locomotives became so filthy during this time. Delivered new on 26 March 1966, D1993 was initially allocated to York (50A). It was renumbered 47291 under the TOPS scheme in March 1974. In November 1995, 47291 (by then in Railfreight grey) collided head-on at Wembley with sister loco 47200, sustaining severe damage to the No. 1 end. It was subsequently withdrawn, but not scrapped until June 2004, at Booth Roe's Rotherham scrapyard. (Charlie Cross)

Virtually 'straight out of the box', Sulzer Type 2 No. D7599 is seen in the company of slightly older, despite what its numbering suggests, sister D7632 at Wath depot in March 1966. D7599 was built at BR Derby works, the second in a line of eighty series 3 (Class 25/3) machines, and was delivered to Tinsley (41A) on 5 February 1966, whereas D7632 came from the Beyer Peacock Gorton works (W/No. 8042) to Tinsley on 8 October 1965. D7599 was renumbered 25249 under the TOPS scheme and, along with three other class members during that day, had the distinction of working the last Class 25 hauled railtour, Hertfordshire Railtours' 'Mersey Ratcatcher' of 28 September 1986. No. 25249 was withdrawn from service on 29 January 1987 and ended up in the 'Sulzer stack' at Vic Berry's scrapyard. D7632 became 25282 under the TOPS scheme and was withdrawn from service on 10 March 1986; by the middle of March 1989 it had been disposed of at Vic Berry's Leicester scrapyard. (Charlie Cross)

Despite having an outrageously short BR career between 1958 and 1967, the Waggon und Maschinenbau German-built railbuses E79962 and M79964 have provided the Worth Valley Railway with many years of service. E79962 was first allocated to Cambridge (31A) for use on East Anglian branch lines such as Marks-Tey–Haverhill/Cambridge, Witham–Maldon and Colchester–Brightlingsea. Resplendent in its two-tone green livery and bearing Worth Valley heraldry and the running number 62, the railbus stands in the shed yard at Haworth on 8 August 1970. It fell into disuse in the 1990s and, now in the ownership of the Vintage Carriages Trust, is the subject of a long-term restoration project.

Depots Old and New

The survival of Immingham's LNER-built coaling tower, even in 1985, was quite remarkable, but thankfully it survives to this day as a listed structure, albeit on private Port of Immingham and railway property. On 11 May 1985, the line-up in the depot yard comprised (from right to left) 37069, 47299, 47295, 47105, 47358 and 47222 *Appleby Frodingham*.

Immingham TMD (IM) on 11 May 1985, with 37002 and 31443 standing alongside the former Great Central Railway (GCR) coaling stage with the LNER-constructed coaling tower visible in the distance. The motive power depot was originally built by the GCR in 1912 to service the newly opened Immingham Docks. Following the splitting of the former BR Trainload business into three sectors in 1994, the depot came under the brief control of the shadow privatisation company Loadhaul before being amalgamated into English, Welsh & Scottish Railway (EWS). After 2009 the servicing of locomotives at Immingham TMD ceased.

No. 40159 of Haymarket depot is stabled with departmental coaches inside the former steam motive power depot at Doncaster on 27 July 1980. Built at the Vulcan Foundry works and delivered new to the Scottish Region in September 1961 as D357, it was withdrawn in July 1983 after failing at Carstairs with a main generator fault, and was disposed of at BREL Doncaster during October 1983.

Romanian-built 56012, with sister 56013 behind, stands at the south end of Doncaster depot on 27 July 1980. Despite the former LNER steam motive power depot having survived for so long, the last locomotives (DB Schenker 66165 and 08993) left the depot on 29 April 2014 prior to its demolition to make way for a new Hitachi Class 800 'Traincare Centre'.

Tinsley TMD on 17 November 1985, with 20139 and other class members present, plus a former steam locomotive tender employed as a water carrier. The depot, along with the marshalling yard, was opened in 1965 and had the capability of handling over 4,000 wagons per day, but it is widely believed to have been outdated before its completion.

A general view of Knottingley TMD on 12 May 1985, with withdrawn 08243 in the foreground and 56117, 56079, 56118, 56003 and others stabled. The depot was strategically situated for easy access to the lines serving the South Yorkshire collieries and the Airedale power stations at Eggborough, Drax and Ferrybridge, the latter visible in the background.

Thirty years ago an amazing variety of classic traction could be seen at Tinsley, with class 08s, 20s, 31s, 37s, 47s and 56s much in evidence in this frosty morning scene on 17 November 1985.

Tinsley TMD yard is seen from the strategically located 'nature trail' path alongside the depot on a splendid crisp and frosty morning on 17 November 1985. In the yard are 47213, large-logo 37410, 37249, 08500 and 08878. There are also several class 20s and a 56 on the back roads.

Class 20 Miscellany

Class 20s 8303 (later 20203), 8305 (later 20205) and behind 8308 (later 20208) stand within the decrepit remains of York motive power depot on 22 March 1970, the site of today's National Railway Museum. No. 8305 (on the right), withdrawn from BR service in December 1989, is still with us today and is preserved by the Class 20 Locomotive Society at the Midland Railway Centre as 20907. (www.railphotoprints.co.uk)

Class 20 D8107 (20107), then on hire from RMS Locotec, awaits its day's duties on an early July morning in 1995 at Flixborough Wharf, Humberside. The locomotive worked the short British Steel branch line between BR Dragonby Sidings and the Faber Prest Steel Terminal wharf located on the east bank of the River Trent.

Ex-works Hunslet Barclay Class 20/9s 20903 *Alison* (BR D8083/20083) and 20902 *Lorna* (BR D8060/20060) outside Doncaster works in May 1997, prior to taking up network weed-killing spray train duties. Both were subsequently acquired by DRS to augment their Class 20/3 fleet for a short period, and travelled to Kosovo in 1999 in the 'Train for Life' charity operation. No. 20902 was scrapped at EMR Kingsbury during September 2011, and 20903 survives, purchased privately by Michael Owen.

Ex-BR Class 20 20056 (ex-D8056), now a Harry Needle Railroad Company (HNRC) hire loco and bearing the TATA Scunthorpe Steelworks running number 81, moves a short load within the Appleby-Frodingham steelworks complex during 2014.

HNRC 20066 (ex-D8066), on hire to Tata Scunthorpe Steelworks and bearing the internal fleet running number 82, shortly after delivery to the works. During 2010 it was overhauled and repainted at Barrow Hill in the striking TATA blue livery, and placed on long-term hire along with 20056.

On the beautiful spring morning of 24 April 1985, a single Class 20, No. 20214, is stabled with an independent snowplough at Tinsley, high above the marshalling yard. Delivered new in May 1967 as D8314 to the North Eastern Region, it served finally at Thornaby from where it was acquired for use on the Lakeside & Haverthwaite Railway.

A crisp frosty morning at Sheffield Midland on 17 November 1985 found 20083 and 20068 on an engineer's working as 31455 arrived on a Trans-Pennine service via the Hope Valley.

The loco-hauled services in support of the Tour de France were extraordinary, and this one was no exception. The 1Q99 06.30 York–Leeds, Harrogate and return to Leeds with DRS 20303 and 20305 (with ex-BR Mk 1 'BG', now VSOE baggage car 92904, sandwiched between) whistles through Cross Gates on the outskirts of Leeds three minutes early at 06.58 on Sunday 6 July 2014. The purpose of this curious working was to convey and deliver Network Rail emergency equipment, the widespread road closures in force preventing a timely road response if necessary.

Nos 20162 and 20068 head a short 'Speedlink' service through York station on 5 June 1985. No. 20162 was withdrawn in November 1987 after just over twenty-one years' service on BR, and 20068 in July 1987 after twenty-six years' service.

Royal Mail and Parcels

Large-logo-liveried 47444 *University of Nottingham* pauses at York heading the down 1L42 parcel vans on 3 June 1987. No. 47444 was built at BR Crewe works as D1560, and entered traffic on 11 March 1964. It was named at Nottingham station by Sir Gordon Hobday, Chancellor of the University of Nottingham, on 14 May 1981. Withdrawn from service during 1994, it was disposed of in July 1995 by M. R. J. Phillips at Crewe works.

Class 55 Deltic 55017 *The Durham Light Infantry* pauses beneath the splendid overall roof at York at 17.15 on 25 November 1981, heading a King's Cross–Newcastle semi-fast service, picking up mail sacks in the process. This class member was unique in that it was devoid of the footstep cut-out on the nose, following collision repairs undertaken late in its career. It was the last Deltic to have a power unit change at Doncaster works, and was filmed by the BBC. The locomotive worked the last regular service diagrammed for a Deltic out of King's Cross on 31 December 1981, the 16.03 for York.

Against a threatening sky, 31305 heads the celebrated 4M19 13.05 Heaton–Red Bank empty parcels wagons at Peckfield in March 1988. This was a keenly followed service, the empty parcels vans, sometimes incredibly long trailing loads, being returned from the north-east to Manchester for reloading with newspapers and parcels during the following evening. The last service ran on 11 July 1988. (Adrian Freeman)

BR Class 40 40160 heads the 4M19 13.05 Heaton–Red Bank parcels empties at Standedge Tunnel, Marsden, in September 1984. The venerable English Electric machine, introduced to BR Scottish Region service in October 1961 as D360, was to be withdrawn from service just two months later. (Adrian Freeman)

BR Class 45 Peak 45059 (previously named *Royal Engineer*) in charge of the 21.50 York–Shrewsbury 'subsidiary service' Travelling Post Office (TPO) at York station on 25 November 1981. There was passenger accommodation available on this service until the May 1988 timetable change.

BR Class 46 Peak 46045, heading a Down parcels service in the early hours at York on 26 July 1980. Fifty-six Class 46 locomotives were built at Derby works, between 1962 and 1963, with D182 entering traffic in 1962, allocated to Gateshead. It was to remain there throughout its main-line career of twenty-two years. A lack of electric train heating equipment meant that class withdrawal commenced in 1978; however 46045 was to be one of the last survivors and was not withdrawn until November 1984, after failing on an Exeter–Severn Tunnel Junction freight service. It was subsequently transferred into departmental stock, being allocated the number 97404, used as a traction unit for wheel adhesion tests and based at the Derby Railway Technical Centre (RTC). As a result, 46045 made it into preservation and is owned by the Peak Locomotive Company and kept at the Midland Railway Centre.

York–Malton–Scarborough

No. 25279, standing at Platform 4 at York heading the 18.53 service to Scarborough on 5 June 1985. Built by Beyer-Peacock at Gorton works, Manchester, just before the company went into liquidation, it was introduced into BR service as D7629 in September 1965 and allocated to Wath for hauling inter-regional freights between the Eastern and Midland Regions of BR. At the time of its withdrawal in March 1987 it was one of the last of its class in service. It was purchased for preservation in 1987 from Vic Berry's Leicester scrapyard and can now be found at the Great Central Railway (North) at Ruddington.

Metro-Cammell (later Class 101) DMU E50257 and its trailer, forming a Malton–Whitby via Pickering service at Malton on 2 January 1965. The 'speed-whiskers' on such units had by this time been replaced by a more conspicuous yellow warning panel. The Malton–Whitby service was ended in March 1965 as part of the 'Beeching Axe'. (Chris Davies/www.railphotoprints.co.uk)

BR Doncaster-built 03073 struggles to move the empty stock of the Wakefield service out of Platform 1 at Scarborough on 18 June 1983. This Class 03 found its way to the Wirral for duties at Birkenhead, where it ended its BR service. It can now be found at the Crewe Heritage Centre. (John Chalcraft/www.railphotoprints.co.uk)

Northallerton

EWS Grid 56115 heading away from the East Coast Main Line at Northallerton near Brompton-on-Swale in charge of the 6N30 Scunthorpe–Lackenby steel slabs on 12 August 1999. This was one of thirty-three stored ex-EWS Class 56s disposed of by DB Schenker in 2011, subsequently being purchased by Europhoenix for export to the Hungarian freight operator Floyd.

The 'Harrogate Loop'

The driver of RES-liveried 47774 *Post Restante*, heading a Leeds–Edinburgh 'Green Express' charter on 4 April 1999, gives up to the Railtrack signalman at Cattal the single line token for the section from Knaresborough. The Class 47, new to Old Oak Common depot as D1746 in July 1964, was to enjoy three further years of main-line service and, after a period of storage, was disposed of at Crewe depot in March 2006.

The signalman offers the single line token for the section to Cattal as Longsight's 40145 approaches Knaresborough station heading a BR (Eastern Region)-sponsored York Circular railtour on Sunday 13 August 1978. The locomotive survives in preservation, and made a welcome main-line comeback in June 2014.

DRS 47810 *Peter Bath MBE*, on the rear of the late-running 19.37 Leeds–Harrogate 'Le Grand Départ' extra, glints in the low evening sun as it crosses the River Aire on the Kirkstall viaduct at Armley, Leeds, on Saturday 5 July 2014.

Knaresborough station is a splendid survivor on our national network, and oozes with atmosphere, especially at night, but loco-hauled passenger services are now very few and far between. DB Schenker 67006 *Royal Sovereign* passes through the well-maintained station at 22.21 on Saturday 5 July 2014, heading a Leeds–York 'Le Grand Départ' limited-stop extra passenger service, providing a rare opportunity to witness a loco-hauled service on the route.

Metropolitan-Cammell Class 101 DMU unit nos 50161, 59306, 59075 and 50638 stand in the Harrogate bay platform at York on 26 July 1980.

A Leeds–Knaresborough service formed of Metropolitan-Cammell Class 101 unit nos 51526 and 51191 leaves Harrogate during the evening of 29 May 1989.

DMU Miscellany

The Class 141 Leyland Second Generation DMUs were arguably the most rudimentary multiple units constructed for use on BR, but York station looks no less majestic with one in its presence. Un-rebuilt unit 141003 (55505–55525) forms a Selby service, as a TPO service stands in the Up Platform 3 during the late evening of 3 June 1987. As older units were becoming life-expired, BR engineers appraised the Leyland National bus, then in widespread usage and with a basic modular design, as a basis for a cost-effective DMU solution. Several single and two-car prototypes were built and tested before an order was ultimately placed in 1984 with Leyland Bus for twenty Class 141 two-car units. The 141s were notoriously unreliable, but reliability improved when they were modified by Hunslet-Barclay between 1988 and 1989. They were based mainly in and across West Yorkshire on routes radiating from Leeds, where they worked up until 1997, when finally replaced by Class 142s. Sponsored by West Yorkshire Passenger Transport Executive (WYPTE), they were initially painted in the Executive's Verona green and buttermilk livery with 'MetroTrain' branding, as in this photograph, but later received the red and cream 'Metro-Train' livery. This unit, along with eleven others, was exported to Iran. They operated in the UK for fourteen years, and in Iran the lifespan was just eight years, making a total of twenty-two years for an extremely basic and rough-riding vehicle.

A Lincoln-allocated and 1956-built Class 114 Derby Heavyweight twin, unit nos 50006 and 56036, stands in the bay Platform 11 at York forming the 22.18 departure to Sheffield on 25 November 1981. The forty-nine Derby twin sets based at Lincoln were a common sight over a wide area bounded by Lincoln, Doncaster, Sheffield, Spalding, Louth, Skegness, Cleethorpes, Scunthorpe and York, and they even worked diagrams over the Hope Valley line to Manchester.

A Class 123 Swindon-built InterCity four-car set working a Trans-Pennine service across the Selby swing bridge on 28 July 1983. (Graham Roose)

BR-built Class 123 Inter City DMU E52100 at Hull Botanic Gardens in July 1984. The InterCity sets were built by BR Swindon works in 1963, and bore a resemblance to the Class 309 Clacton Express EMUs built at York just before these units emerged from Swindon works, the final batch of first-generation units to be built. They saw out their final years augmenting the Class 124 Trans-Pennine sets on the Hull–Doncaster–Sheffield–Manchester and occasionally Leeds route before final withdrawal came in May 1984. No vehicles survive in preservation. (www.railphotoprints.co.uk)

A Swindon-built Trans-Pennine Class 124 set gets a close inspection at York, on 23 July 1967. A distinctive feature of the Class 124 driving units, very similar to the Glasgow 'Blue Train' Class 303 EMUs, was the stylish wrap-around window design. The units were withdrawn from service in May 1984 and none have survived in preservation. (Chris Davies/www.railphotoprints.co.uk)

Calder Valley unit 52083, 59703 and 51814 stabled in the roofless depot at Bradford Hammerton Street on 10 November 1979. Introduced in 1960, the distinctive BRCW Class 110 units were built specifically for the steeply graded Calder Valley line across the Pennines.

Class 105 Cravens two-car unit 54472 and 51276, the last of two such sets working from Lincoln depot at this time, was forming a service to Lincoln at Doncaster on 5 June 1985. The two large windows of the Sheffield-built Cravens units were distinctive.

Class 108 Derby Lightweight unit 53964 and 54247 stands at Huddersfield on 28 May 1991. The unit was repainted into 'retro' BR green livery for an open day at Carlisle Currock in 1986. The vehicles had alloy bodies with steel ends in the style of the all-steel vehicles built at Derby, and production of the units continued through to 1961.

Class 110 unit 51841, 59813 and 51819 forming a Manchester Victoria–Leeds service at Hebden Bridge on 15 June 1981. The BRCW Class 110 was the final private build of first-generation units, essentially an updated version of the Class 104s but with a redesigned front cab. They entered traffic in January 1962 and were used on the former Lancashire & Yorkshire main line, which earned them the name 'Calder Valley' sets. (Author's Collection, photographer Graham Roose)

A Class 108 Derby Lightweight unit (with DTCL unit No. 56208 trailing) stands at the listed and then gaslit Victorian station at Ilkley on 14 June 1977, forming a service to Leeds. These units were built without asbestos insulation and were an early choice in the BR refurbishment programme of the mid- to late 1970s when units were out-shopped in the short-lived white/blue stripe livery, which included a brown underframe. (Author's Collection, photographer Graham Roose)

Under the Wires

With just over two weeks to go before closure of the Woodhead route, 76040 leans to the curve at Shore Hill, Thurlstone, with a short unfitted train of mineral wagons on 29 June 1981. (Author's Collection, photographer Graham Roose)

A tremendous line-up of EM1 DC electric locos at Wath depot on 16 July 1967, with E26020 at the head of the row, and numerous English Electric Type 3s (later Class 37) also visible in the background. Wath marshalling yard was built by the Great Central Railway at the turn of the century and was situated in the centre of the South Yorkshire coalfield. (Author's Collection, photographer Mike Blenkinsop)

Class EM2 27000 *Electra* at Sheffield Victoria in 1968. The Woodhead route was electrified by the LNER as early as 1939 at 1,500-volt DC overhead, but electrification between Manchester and Sheffield was not completed until 1955; it was extended to the then new Tinsley marshalling yard in 1965. Sheffield Victoria station was closed two years after this photograph was taken. (the late Colin Whitfield/www.railphotoprints.co.uk)

E26050 (formerly named *Stentor*) is at the head of a row of Class EM1 1,500 DC electric locomotives at Wath Depot on 11 April 1971, with 26053 (formerly named *Perseus*) behind. E26050 unusually had a BR totem applied to the standard BR blue livery.

In a scene now quite incredulous, passengers from the 'Pennine Rambler' railtour of 7 October 1978 spill out from the platform on to the running lines to photograph 76010 and 76023 during its sixteen-minute pause at Penistone station. (Author's Collection)

With York Minster standing prominently on the horizon and rain falling over the city of York, EWS 86416 and 90026 speed the Low Fell–Plymouth Royal Mail postal service south near Colton Junction on 6 July 1999.

A GNER Edinburgh–King's Cross service working on the Down line at Great Heck, passing the Plasmor Ltd works on 25 August 2000. The Plasmor concrete block manufacturing works' private siding is to the right, with the John Fowler 0-4-0 diesel hydraulic shunter (W/No. 4220038, built in 1966) waiting at the headshunt for the incoming train of empty wagons from Bow. It was at this location some six months later that the tragic Great Heck rail disaster occurred on the morning of 28 February 2001. Ten people died, including the drivers of both trains involved, and eighty-two people suffered serious injuries. It remains the worst rail disaster of the twenty-first century in the United Kingdom.

The unique 89001 designed by Brush Traction, heading the 15.40 London King's Cross–Bradford Forster Square, at Beeston in June 1997. It was built at BREL Crewe in 1986 as a potential replacement for the Class 86, and was the only one of its type. It suffered an unacceptable number of in-service failures and was withdrawn in 1992. Rescued by a group of staff from Brush works, it was eventually purchased by GNER and brought back up to main-line standard to augment the fleet of class 91s. Driver knowledge saw it restricted mainly to the Yorkshire services, and its end of service on the main line came in 2000 when it suffered a traction motor failure and was eventually deemed surplus to the requirements of GNER. (Adrian Freeman)

The West Yorkshire Passenger Transport Executive acquired a number of class 307s from Network South East for use on the Leeds–Doncaster local services. No. 307102 was photographed forming the 18.28 Doncaster service at Leeds in August 1991; it retained its NSE colours throughout its short period of service in Yorkshire, prior to the arrival of the class 321 units. (Adrian Freeman)

The unique prototype 89001 is seen at Leeds heading the 'Thames Eden Limited' railtour in January 1989, before it was named *Avocet* later that year. Now in the care of the AC Locomotive Group, it is kept at Barrow Hill and bears the original InterCity livery once more, although electrical restoration is still a lengthy ongoing process. (Adrian Freeman)

Class 91 No. 91002, hauling an HST set 'slab end', first departing Leeds for London King's Cross on 29 May 1989. The first ten of the class were built at BREL Crewe in 1988 and were designed to be tilting, with a top speed of 140 mph. Before the Mk 4 coaches and DVTs were delivered, a number of HST power cars were converted to act as surrogate DVTs, with Mk 3 carriages being used. If the locomotives are operated 'slab end', the maximum line speed is reduced to 110 mph. The class received a major refurbishment between 2000 and 2002, and was consequently reclassified 91/1.

The Leeds–Settle–Carlisle Line

Class 47/0 47077 *North Star* departing from Leeds at 12.30 heading a Newcastle–Swansea service on 10 November 1979. The Brush Type 4 was introduced to BR service as D1661 in February 1965 and was allocated to Landore. It was withdrawn from main-line service in February 2007 as 47840, and was the final class 47 in a batch of Virgin locos to be given retro liveries in 2002, being turned out in the once unpopular BR blue livery by popular demand from enthusiasts.

A Class 308 unit forming a Skipton–Bradford service at a flooded Cononley in November 2000, during its last months of service. Upon electrification of the Leeds–Bradford–Skipton and Ilkley lines in 1994–95 no new stock was procured; instead, BR decided to overhaul displaced Class 308 units from the London–Tilbury–Southend line at Doncaster works as a cost-effective solution. The formations were reduced from four to three carriages, which were turned out in the West Yorkshire 'Metro-Train' maroon and cream livery. By the late 1990s it was clear that the elderly units were life-expired, being increasingly unreliable and expensive to maintain. They were replaced by sixteen new four-car Class 333 units, built by Siemens in Germany, which were introduced from 1999. (Adrian Freeman)

Renovation and rebuilding of Skipton station prior to electrification had just commenced when this photograph was taken in April 1994. It shows Regional Railways Derby works 1986-built Pacer unit 144007 forming a stopping service to Shipley and Bradford.

Holbeck-allocated Peak D23 (later 45017) heads the 1M91 Up 'Waverley', still with the nameboards on the coaches, through the remains of the closed station at Kildwick & Crosshills, between Skipton and Keighley, in September 1967. (Author's Collection)

On 6 June 2014 the Class 40 Preservation Society's 345 (40145) is glimpsed through an interconnecting passage between the island platforms at Hellifield station as it heads the 1Z28 13.14 Carnforth–Bury positioning special non-stop through the station.

Deltic Class 55 55015 *Tulyar* pauses at Hellifield working the BR-organised 'Hadrian Flyer', the 1Z35 from Peterborough to Carlisle on 5 December 1981, which had originated from King's Cross at 02.00 and travelled via Spalding, Lincoln, Doncaster, Normanton and the S&C to Carlisle, Newcastle, Doncaster, Lincoln and Peterborough, all for the princely sum of £12 (adult) or £5 (child). (Author's Collection)

A Virgin Cross Country HST, with power car 43097 leading, diverted via the Settle–Carlisle route, and seen against the stunning late afternoon sunlit snow-capped backdrop of Penyghent at Selside on 3 March 2001.

Large logo-liveried 47519 in Monastral blue large-logo livery heads the 'Settle Carlisle Thunderer' railtour, northbound off Ribblehead viaduct and approaching Blea Moor signal box on Saturday 26 February 1994. Built at BR Crewe works and first allocated to York, it carried the pre-TOPS number D1102. It ended its days in BR two-tone green livery and was scrapped by T. J. Thomson at Stockton in October 2005. (Author's Collection)

RES-liveried 47565 *Responsive* heads the 1Z09 08.00 'Lothian Fellsman' railtour from Edinburgh Waverley and return via the Settle & Carlisle Railway on 19 March 1994. The Cheshire Railtours charter, with eleven InterCity-liveried coaches, is seen heading south off the Ribblehead viaduct with the snow-capped bulk of Whernside looming behind. New in September 1964 to Toton depot as D1620, it survived in service for almost forty years, finally meeting its fate like many others, at Booth Roe's Rotherham scrapyard in February 2004. (Author's Collection)

Substituting for the failed Stanier Class 8F 2-8-0 steam locomotive, Stratford 47 Group's 47580 *County of Essex*, bearing the Union Flag on its body sides, heads the 1Z53 15.34 Carlisle–Lancaster return 'Fellsman' on 25 June 2014. The locomotive has put in a good mileage during the 2014 main-line steam season, substituting for, or as assisting power during the FBU strike and fire risk period of the summer season of steam charters.

The one and only run of the 'Minimodal' concept of containerised freight over the Settle & Carlisle line ran on 28 August 2002, and was photographed heading off Dandry Mire viaduct at Garsdale. DRS Cromptons 33030 and 33025 top and tail the Megafret twin wagon, conveying twelve cube containers in connection with a marketing filming sequence for the prototype concept taking place at Settle station. The BRCW Type 3 1,550 hp Bo-Bo design for the Southern Region was equipped with both vacuum and air brakes, and had driving positions on both sides of each cab. Members of the class during their early years worked in tandem on the weekly Cliffe–Uddingston block cement train, at least as far north as York.

Heritage Railways

No. 20020 of the Wensleydale Railway heads a Leeming Bar–Redmire service away from Wensley on 30 August 2010. The Wensleydale Railway Association was formed in 1990 with the aim of reinstating the 19 miles between Garsdale and Redmire, then eventually going on to Northallerton. Twenty-five years on, services now run over a section of the route and it remains an ambition to rebuild west from Redmire towards Garsdale, connecting with the Settle–Carlisle line.

Class 31/1 31128 *Charybdis* stabled with its stock in the loop at Whitby harbour before working the return morning service to Grosmont and Pickering on the North Yorkshire Moors Railway (NYMR) on 12 August 2010. The Brush Type 2 was delivered from Falcon works, Loughborough, to BR in August 1959 as D5546, and was initially allocated to Ipswich depot. Following withdrawal by EWS it was sold in 2000, initially to Fragonset, but following the demise of this operator it was acquired by Nemesis Rail and kept at Barrow Hill. In June 2010 it was loaned to the NYMR, being certified to operate their services over Network Rail infrastructure.

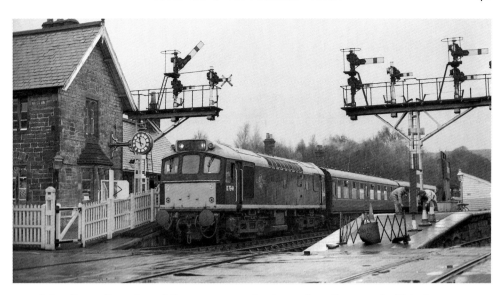

Sulzer Type 2 (later class 25) D7541 prepares to head away from Grosmont for Pickering on 13 November 1998. D7541 was built at BR Derby works and first allocated to Toton in April 1965. As a London Midland Region locomotive it was allocated to various depots before arriving at Crewe diesel depot in 1986. It was officially withdrawn on 18 March 1987, bearing the TOPS number 25191, and was purchased for use on the NYMR, losing its BR blue livery and TOPS number in favour of the more attractive BR two-tone green livery. In 1992 it regained its original number and the name *The Diana* after the wife of Lord Downe. It eventually fell out of use and was subsequently purchased for use on the South Devon Railway in April 2011.

Recreating an early 1960s scene, Sulzer Type 2s (later Class 24) D5061 and D5032 (TOPS 24061 and 24032 respectively) tackle the steep ascent into Goathland station with gusto, but not without noise, heading a demonstration freight at the NYMR diesel gala day on 15 November 1998.

South Yorkshire

Railfreight grey-liveried 31116 arrives at Sheffield with a service from Manchester on 4 June 1987, with 47594 stabled beyond. No. 31116 was introduced into service with BR Eastern Region in June 1959 as D5534, and was withdrawn from service in January 1995.

An early morning scene at Sheffield Midland station on 16 March 1985, with HST power car No. 43017 flanked by Class 110 BRCW Calder Valley and Class 114 Derby units.

It is 00.45 by the Doncaster station clock, and Peak Class 46 No. 46016 waits for departure on the 00.57 Leeds–Paignton sleeper service on 26 July 1980. Delivered new from BR Derby works in January 1962 as D153, it saw a short period of storage at Swindon works in late 1980, but was soon reinstated and transferred to Gateshead, where it was a regular performer on the NE/SW route. It was finally withdrawn from service in December 1983 and disposed of at Swindon during August 1984.

The entire Class 50 fleet received heavy overhaul at Doncaster from 1979. Resplendent in its fresh coat of paint, 50010 *Monarch* heads the Doncaster works test train away from Sheffield on its proving run on 24 April 1985. Class 45/1 Peak No. 45142 stands alongside.

Shunting Locomotives

Goole (50D) had three North British shunters on its books, D2700–D2702, in the 1950s/1960s for shunting the docks, and locos of the same design were also supplied to the Ministry of Defence Army Department between 1955 and 1959. Surplus to requirements, Army 0-4-0 diesel hydraulic shunters 408 (North British W/No. 27429, built in 1955) and 409 (North British W/No. 27644, built in 1959) found their way to Yorkshire and await cutting up at Marple & Gillott's Attercliffe scrapyard on 5 June 1985. The works Vanguard shunter, built by Thomas Hill (W/No. 140V, built in 1964), stands behind.

Innumerable locomotives and rail vehicles of both BR and industrial origin have been disposed of at the Booth Roe (formerly C. F. Booth Ltd) Rotherham scrapyard. Offering a flavour of the diversity to be found, on a visit made on 12 February 1993, this line-up was seen from the strategic public access thoroughfare, which included *Enterprise*, an 0-6-0 diesel mechanical built by Hudswell Clarke in 1953 (W/No. D810), 47456, 08334 and an ex-NCB Shirebrook 0-4-0 diesel hydraulic built by Hudswell Clarke (W/No. D1344, built in 1965).

D0226 *Vulcan* in the shed yard at Haworth, Keighley & Worth Valley Railway, on 9 August 1970. One of two (D0226 and D0227) prototype diesel shunting locomotives built in 1956 by English Electric at its Vulcan Foundry in Newton-le-Willows as demonstration locos for BR, D0226 has diesel-electric transmission and D0227 had diesel-hydraulic transmission. BR tested both locomotives at its Stratford depot in east London, but the design was not perpetuated. D0227 was scrapped in 1960 and D0226 eventually entered preservation as the only surviving prototype BR main-line shunting locomotive in existence.

There was much variety in the types of small shunter supplied to BR, and the Barclay-built examples were no exception. BR Departmental 0-4-0 diesel mechanical No. 81, built by Andrew Barclay (W/No. 424) in 1958, was photographed at Doncaster in June 1966. Withdrawn from BR service in November 1967 as the 'second' D2956, just before being allocated a class 01 TOPS number, it was scrapped by Duport Steel at Briton Ferry in August 1969. (Charlie Cross)

A line-up of fully restored shunting locomotives at the Appleby Frodingham Railway Preservation Society's shed within the TATA Scunthorpe Steelworks complex in August 2014, with Yorkshire Engine Co. Class 02 D2853 (W/No. 2812, built in 1960), numbered 02003 under the TOPS scheme, a Yorkshire Engine Co. Janus locomotive, *Appleby Frodingham 1* (W/No. 2877, built in 1963), and Ruston Paxman Class 07 0-6-0 diesel electric 07012 (Ruston & Hornsby W/No. 480697, built in 1962), numbered D2996 under the TOPS scheme. The Class 02 and 07s were built for dock shunting in Merseyside and Southampton respectively, but neither class is generally associated with the region. However, a visit made by the author to Goole depot in April 1968 found D2859 and D2865 present.

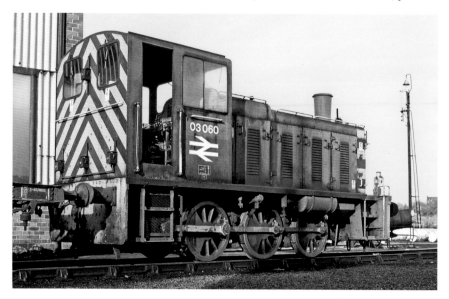

Class 03 0-6-0 diesel mechanical No. 03060 stands outside Bradford Hammerston Street depot on 10 November 1979. Originally built as D2060 at BR Doncaster works, it entered traffic in June 1959, initially allocated to Gateshead depot. A transfer to Colchester came in March 1971, followed in 1977 by one to Hammerton Street, for use primarily on pilot duties at Exchange station. Withdrawal came in December 1982, and during July 1983 it was cut up at BREL Doncaster works, where numerous other class members were disposed of.

Coming under the jurisdiction of the South Yorkshire Area of the NCB, although just in North Nottinghamshire, Manton Colliery near Worksop possessed an ex-BR Drewry class 04. D2229 was representative of a number of ex-BR class 04s that found their way into Yorkshire collieries, and was photographed on 14 June 1987 alongside No. 20 *Manton*, a Hudswell Clark 0-6-0 diesel mechanical (W/No. D1121, built in 1958), in the BR exchange sidings serving the colliery. D2229 was withdrawn from BR service at Thornaby in December 1969 and was sold to the NCB, initially working at Orgreave and Brookhouse collieries before moving on to Manton. Two members of the class, D2245 and D2298, also found use after BR service between 1969 and 1978 on the private freight-only Derwent Valley Light Railway near York.

The daily BR 'wagonload' pick-up goods service to the Allied Steel & Wire Ltd private sidings at Meadowhall, diagrammed for Tinsley-allocated Class 08 No. 08870, has split the points and derailed. It awaits a BR re-railing team on 24 April 1985. The building behind was originally part of the works for the Yorkshire Engine Company, a small independent locomotive manufacturer in Sheffield mainly known for shunting engines for the British market, including the BR class 02, but it also built main-line engines for overseas customers. The company was formed in 1865, and continued to produce locomotives and carry out general engineering work until 1965.

Over 1,100 350/400 hp English Electric 0-6-0 diesel electric shunters were built, most being limited to 20 mph to maximise tractive effort. EWS-liveried 08888 was stabled in Trent Sidings, Scunthorpe, in June 2011. It had previously worked at Margam and Cardiff Tidal yards and had not long been transferred to Scunthorpe upon completion of the DB Schenker shunting contract at Cardiff. The former BR D4118 was new to Swindon shed in February 1962. It was the subject of a pilot trial at Mossend yard in 2010, trialling remote control equipment with a view to making reductions among the ground staff, but proved to be unsuccessful due to its poor transmitter range and incompatible speed control unit, though it did gain the nickname 'Robbie the Robot' in the process.

A number of both ex-BR and industrial locomotives could be seen at the Booth Roe Metals Rotherham scrapyard on 22 May 1989. Class 11 No. 12099 was introduced into service from BR Derby works in March 1952 and saw use at many LMR depots, including Nottingham and Willesden, before joining the NCB fleet, visiting Wales and Yorkshire prior to reaching the Rotherham scrapyard, where it is seen here shortly after arrival from Bowers Row disposal point, near Castleford, in the company of an ex-NCB Rolls-Royce 0-6-0 diesel hydraulic (W/No. 10257, built in 1966). No. 12099 was sold on to the Severn Valley Railway in 1990 and is usually employed as the Kidderminster yard shunter. A batch of Class 11 shunters (12113–12122) were allocated to Hull Alexandra Dock shed for shunting the extensive dock lines, but all were withdrawn from service by May 1971, 12121 coincidentally being disposed of at this scrapyard in April 1972.

BR green-liveried Master and Slave Class 13 No. D4500 is seen at Tinsley marshalling yard on 11 April 1971. Formed from Class 08 shunters D4188 (master) and D3698 (slave), and introduced in May 1965, this was the first of three special locomotives that were formed by permanently coupling two class 08s together, one with its cab removed, and built specifically for shunting the humps at Sheffield Tinsley yard. The loco retaining the cab is the master and the other the slave. Both units were ballasted to improve traction. Initially they were coupled cab to cab but this was soon found to be impractical. D4500 was renumbered 13003 under the TOPS scheme and lasted until the closure of the Tinsley yard hump in 1985. It was cut up at BREL Doncaster works in September 1986.

During the author's visit to Hull Dairycoates (50B) on 7 April 1968, there were no fewer than thirty-two Class 14 locomotives present, many arranged around the turntable in the former steam motive power depot roundhouse. Following rejection by BR Western Region they were transferred to Hull in order to work trip freights from the docks and mineral traffic between Hessle Quarry and Wilmington cement works for an extremely short period, between 1966 and 1968 before sale into industry or for scrap. Having an average service life on BR of only four years, photographs of the Class 14s in active service are comparatively rare. Even rarer are photographs of them working in Humberside. This photograph, taken in around 1967, is of two class members heading empty Presflo wagons for the cement works, and was hurriedly captured from the front of a Hull-bound DMU skirting the Humber River at Hessle. (Author's Collection)

Workshops and Scrapyards

You could be forgiven for thinking that this varied line-up of traction was arranged in conjunction with some form of an official works open day, but in fact this was just what could be found at Doncaster works on a routine visit on 12 May 1985. It is a quite remarkably varied display of traction, mostly awaiting disposal, with (from left to right) 46028, 08369, 08269, 40025 *Lusitania*, 46046, 58007, 08330, 50012 *Benbow* and 13003.

A closer view of the same scene as above, with 46028, 08269, 08369, 40025 *Lusitania*, 46046 and 58007.

A glimpse through the doorway into the workshops at the 'Doncaster plant' on 27 July 1980 found 50030 *Repulse*, 56009 and 31112. How exciting works visits could be, not knowing what might be found within!

Class 31/0 Toffee Apples 31015 and 31006 await the cutter's torch at BREL Doncaster works on 27 July 1980. These locomotives were two of the original batch of twenty pilot scheme locomotives ordered as part of BR's Modernisation Plan, and were numbered D5515 and D5506 respectively.

Class 50 Hoovers 50003 *Temeraire*, 50038 *Formidable* and 50004 *St. Vincent* are under full revision at Doncaster works 'plant' on 27 July 1980.

Class 56 No. 56084 is seen under construction at BREL Doncaster works on 27 July 1980. This was the first class 56 to emerge in the new BR 'Large Logo' livery, although 56036 received the livery experimentally in the late 1970s. After being accepted into traffic on 26 November 1980, allocated to Tinsley depot, it worked for just eighteen months before being involved in a collision and sent back to the works for heavy repairs.

Fresh from a heavy overhaul and repaint from its BR blue livery, Bristol Bath Road-allocated 56034 stands outside the paint shop at Doncaster 'plant' on 12 May 1985, resplendent in its Railfreight grey livery and before receiving its name, *Castell Ogwr/Ogmore Castle*. Built at BREL Doncaster and introduced into service in August 1977, it wore the Loadhaul sector livery before its final withdrawal came in November 1999; however, it was not disposed of until November 2007 at Booth Roe's Rotherham scrapyard.

Outside Doncaster works on 12 May 1985 were 40135, 08392 and 08248, with 31461 stabled beyond. No. 40135 was from a batch of twenty (D325–D344) built with 'split-box' type headcode. It avoided a very close call with the scrap man at Doncaster, and was one of four class members returned to departmental traffic in May 1985 for use in the remodelling of Crewe station approaches. Based at Crewe TMD, it was renumbered 97406 and worked on various freight duties in the London Midland Region. Final withdrawal from BR service came in December 1986, but happily it was acquired by the Class 40 Preservation Society and can now be found as D335 on the East Lancashire Railway.

No. 37028 is seen receiving a heavy repair in Doncaster works on 27 July 1980. It was released from English Electric Vulcan Foundry in December 1961 as D6728 and initially allocated to Stratford depot.

Withdrawn in December 2000 as 37505 *British Steel Workington*, it was purchased for preservation from T. J. Thomson's Stockton scrapyard in August 2007 and moved to the Eden Valley Railway, where little work was carried out. It was eventually sent for scrap at European Metals Recycling (EMR), Kingsbury, in February 2008 in a swap deal for another class 37.

Regional Railways unit 323 221 is standing outside at Hunslet TPL, Jack Lane works, Leeds, on 21 January 1994. The Class 323 fleet, of which there were forty-three in number, was built between 1992 and 1993, to provide a new set of EMUs for the Cross City electrification project in Birmingham, and to replace the ageing first-generation EMUs operating in the Greater Manchester area. However, teething troubles caused major problems before the fleet were introduced, and sadly they were the last vehicles built before Hunslet at Leeds collapsed, the company having been founded in 1864.

Taking on more of an appearance of a scrapyard than a locomotive repair facility, the yard of RFS Engineering Ltd at Kilnhurst, visited in the winter afternoon sunshine of 24 January 1990, produced an ex-NCB Baddesley Colliery Rolls-Royce Sentinel (W/No. 10212, built in 1964) and Class 08s 08170 and 08216, along with many other industrial locomotives for repair or parts recovery. Kilnhust works finally closed during 1993 and all stock and work were transferred to RFS's Doncaster works by August 1993.

This unlikely line-up of ex-BR and NCB shunters could be found alongside the Rotherham–Doncaster line at Kilnhurst near Mexborough on 12 February 1992. The striking red-liveried Sentinels (W/Nos 10089, 10118 and 10119, all built in 1962) had been acquired by RFS Ltd from the NCB at Kellingley Colliery for refurbishment and resale to industry. The Class 08 shunters (left to right) 08581, 08416 and 08876 did not fare quite as well. No. 08416 was cut up on site during the August, 08581 saw further use until cut up in September 2000 and 08876 was cut up on site in July 1992.

Departmental No. 97203 had a short life in this guise of 97203 operated by the RTC, based at Derby, for in 1987 the locomotive was written off after having sustained fire damage. It was originally delivered as D5831, subsequently renumbered 31298 under the TOPS scheme and withdrawn from capital stock in July 1986, then from departmental use in May 1987. It is seen here awaiting the cutter's torch at Booth Roe's Rotherham scrapyard on 22 May 1989.

The sad hulk of a once greatly admired East Coast 'racehorse', Class 55 Deltic No. 55012 *Crepello*, captured in its final hours at Doncaster works in September 1981.

Peak Class 46 No. 46032 has been reduced to a shell at BREL Doncaster works on 12 May 1985. Class 03 shunter 03175 has already been dismantled and the cab is finding alternative use as a mess hut.

The partly dismantled hulk of 37209 stands in the yard at Doncaster Carr on 21 July 2002, being cut up by HNRC after a period of ten years in a state of limbo awaiting this final fate. Latterly bearing the BR Monastral blue large-logo livery and unofficially named *Phantom*, it was withdrawn at Tinsley during July 1992. It was delivered new from the Vulcan Foundry in December 1963 as D6909, and was initially allocated to Landore depot. (Author's Collection)

Formerly Tinsley-allocated Class 47/0 47102, unofficially named *Buzzard*, waits in line with Class 47/3 47378 for the cutter's torch at Both Roe's scrapyard, Rotherham, on 7 March 1998. Entering BR service in November 1963 as D1690, it was renumbered under the TOPS scheme in February 1974, receiving the unofficial name at Tinsley in November 1989. By August 1998 it was no more. (Author's Collection)

Booth Roe's scrapyard on 21 June 1992 with Class 50 Hoovers 50036 *Victorious* and 50026 *Indomitable* and the ex-NCB Hudswell Clarke site shunter. No. 50036 was cut up soon after this photograph was taken, although 50026 fared considerably better and was towed away for preservation.

Industrial Counterparts

Many ex-BR locos and multiple units, as well as industrials, were disposed of in the former BR Attercliffe goods depot yard near Sheffield. This was the end of the line for the unique Army 0-8-0 diesel hydraulics built by Andrew Barclay Sons & Co. at Kilmarnock between 1964 and 1966. They are seen awaiting the cutter's torch at Marple & Gillott, Attercliffe, and were photographed in the heavy rain at 7 a.m. on 5 June 1985. These powerful locos worked exclusively on the Kineton and Bicester Military Railways and were rarely photographed. The line-up, with nameplates and running numbers removed/obliterated, comprised (from the front) 624 *Royal Pioneer* (W/No. 504), 622 *Greensleeves* (W/No. 502), 620 *Sapper* (W/No. 500) and 623 *Storeman* (W/No. 503). Unfortunately none of these unique locomotives were rescued for preservation.

Wearing its short-lived striking red livery, the massive RFS-built 150-ton Co-Co diesel-hydraulic shunting locomotive *Cracoe* (W/No. 067/C4498GA/57000/01, built in 1994) is seen at Tilcon's Rylstone Quarry, near Grassington, on the frosty morning of 23 December 1994. This was the final locomotive to be built at the Doncaster works site, just as RFS Doncaster went into receivership. The locomotive design was loosely based on the popular Thomas Hill Ltd 'Steelman' range of industrial locomotives. It is quite fitting that the last standard gauge locomotive built for industry in Yorkshire should remain in the county and furthermore emerge from the famous Doncaster works.

A rarely photographed locomotive and location is the Conoco Ltd Humberside refinery at South Killingholme. In April 1992, newly built and delivered 590 hp six-wheel diesel hydraulic *Earl of Yarborough* was the penultimate locomotive to be built by RFS Ltd (W/No. V336, of 1991) and the last constructed at their Kilnhurst works near Mexborough. A Hunslet 256 hp 0-4-0 diesel hydraulic (W/No. 6981, built in 1968) stands as spare loco in the shed.

Ex-LMS 350 hp and BR Class 11 No. 12083 stands as spare loco at Swinden limeworks on 8 February 1993. Behind can be seen the working loco at the time, ex-BR Class 08 08054 (formerly D3067). No. 12083 arrived at the works after withdrawal from BR service, which took place in October 1971, as a former Carlisle Kingmoor-allocated shunter. It is now to be found on the Battlefield Line in Leicestershire. No. 08054 had been withdrawn from BR in February 1980 and worked at the quarry until 1998. It was donated to the nearby Yorkshire Dales Railway by Tarmac in 2008. The lime kilns towering above the locos continued to burn lime until 1996.

North Yorkshire Branch Lines

Mainline-liveried 37047 and 'Dutch'-liveried 37058 return to Skipton and Reading from Rylstone, heading a Pathfinder Tours 'Summer Symphony' special on the freight-only branch near Cracoe on 17 July 1999.

No. 60096 *Ben Macdui* (bearing the Petroleum Sector decals) powers away from Skipton in the rain on 8 February 1993, heading the Rylstone–Hull loaded with limestone. The train has just come off the former Grassington branch line, the loco having rounded the four-wheel hopper wagons in the Down siding north of the station.

With the temperature not rising above freezing throughout the day and the weak sun failing to thaw the overnight hoar frost, 37716 and 37884 power away from Wensley station with the Black Cat Railtours 1Z36 Crewe–Redmire 'Redmire Farewell Railtour' on 29 December 1992.

Mainline-liveried 37216 with a heavy load of Army light armoured infantry vehicles at Wensley on the Wensleydale branch between Northallerton and Redmire on 3 September 1999. The branch once formed a through route from the NER at Northallerton to the MR at Garsdale, and passenger traffic was withdrawn as early as 1954.

On 3 September 1999, EWS 37893 approaches Wensley station with light armoured vehicles bound for Ludgershall, Wiltshire, from Redmire loading point, following Army infantry exercises on the Catterick training area and ranges.

Simultaneous Class 101 DMU arrivals at the NER-built Battersby Junction station on 23 August 1988, with unit 51515 and 51217 on the left forming an Esk Valley service to Whitby, and on the right unit 51467 and 53240 from Whitby, about to exchange the single line token. The Esk Valley line survived the proposed closure under the Beeching Report of 1963 due to the Government acknowledging that the route provided a vital link through the remotest parts of the North Yorkshire Moors.

Milford and Wakefield Area

Railfreight grey-liveried (without sector decals) 60021 *Pen-y-ghent* rounds the curve between Milford Junction and Gascoigne Wood heading Drax–Immingham empty bogie oil tankers on 13 March 2001. The 'Tug' was repainted in the EWS red and gold livery and named *Star of the East*, continuing in traffic until November 2009. It was one of the many subsequently stored at Toton, but has now been purchased by Colas Railfreight and may well see mainline service once more.

EWS 66094 accelerates past the Gascoigne Wood Colliery loading point on 27 August 1999 heading the 6E01 09.30 Mostyn–Hull Saltend acetic acid empty tankers. Gascoigne Wood was the largest mine in the Selby complex, which was made up of five interconnecting deep mines within a 20-mile area. The Selby complex was to be the largest deep-mining complex in the world; developed during the 1970s, it provided coal for the nearby coal-fired power stations. When opened it heralded the future of deep mining, providing highly efficient secure energy for the future. Under privatisation in 2004 the whole complex was closed and the shafts filled.

EWS 59203 *Vale of Pickering* heading MGR empties for Gascoigne Wood Colliery at South Milford on 2 September 1999. In April 1998 EWS took over the National Power Rail operations. The class 59/2s eventually became more widely deployed around the country under EWS/DB Schenker management, but from 2005 were allocated to work alongside the Mendip Rail fleet based at Merehead depot.

In September 1985, and still bearing evidence of its Stratford white roof, Class 47 47093 of Cardiff depot heads a 'Speedlink' containerised household coal train at Castleford West Junction, comprising 30-foot Russell ISOs on 'FPA' wagons from Markham Main Colliery near Doncaster for eventual delivery to Gartcosh, Aberdeen Guild Street and Inverness Harbour Branch coal depots. The class 47 was to see just two more years of active service, and was finally disposed of at MC Metals, Glasgow, in June 1990. (Author's Collection)

Immingham-allocated 37680 runs through Castleford with the 6E39 09.49 Mostyn–Hull Saltend acetic acid tanks on 20 June 1994. The 'vinegar tank' services from Hull to Mostyn, Spondon and Baglan Bay were regular diagrams for class 37s at this time. No. 37680 (previously D6924 and 37224) was stored between September 2003 and June 2010 under the ownership of EWS and then HNRC, but was disposed of at T. J. Thomson, Stockton, in December 2010.

RES-liveried 47790 *Saint David/Dewi Saint* heads the short EWS 'Enterprise' service trip working from Healey Mills yard to Cobra Railfreight at Wakefield on 23 July 1999. This class 47 is, at the time of writing, still very much active with DRS and resplendent in the 'Northern Belle' livery for exclusive use on their prestigious dining car services.

White-stained Mainline 37248 *Midland Railway Centre* (with 37077 on the rear) disturbs the peace of Horbury and fills the cutting with fumes as it gets into its stride soon after leaving Healey Mills yard with a weed killing train for York and Bridlington on a wet 5 August 1999. No. 37248 (D6948) is now owned by the Growler Group and is currently based on the Gloucestershire & Warwickshire Railway.

No. 37711 (formerly named *Tremorfa Steelworks*) working tube stock from London via Didcot for refurbishment at Bombardier, Horbury Junction, passing through Horbury cutting on 4 August 1999. Originally delivered new in December 1962 as D6785 to Gateshead depot, it was finally withdrawn from service in June 2005 and disposed of in March 2006 at MC Metals, Kingsbury.

EWS Loadhaul-liveried 60008 *Gypsum Queen II* heads the 6M89 09.51 Dewsbury–Earles Sidings empty cement tankers through Horbury cutting on 30 July 1999. Originally named *Moel Fammau* when new, it later received its third name, *Sir William McAlpine*, to accompany its EWS red and gold livery. The loco has latterly been in store at Toton.

EWS 60098 *Charles Francis Brush* is leaving Healey Mills yard with loaded coal in MGRs from Ayrshire on 4 October 1999. There is not a class 66 to be seen in this view, with three class 56s and a 37 stabled, and many stored class 47s, with Railfreight Distribution 47200 at the head of the row.

Right: Mainline grey EWS Class 37 No. 37705 with three vans in tow on a trip working from Healey Mills yard to Cobra Railfreight at Wakefield, passing through the deep sandstone cutting at Horbury on Thursday 5 August 1999. Delivered new in October 1962 as D6760, it was initially allocated to Thornaby depot. In its latter years, after a period of contract hire in France it was repatriated and placed into store, but was officially withdrawn in July 2007 and cut up the following month by T. J. Thomson of Stockton.

Below: With 'Ferry Vans' originating on the overnight 'Enterprise' service from Wembley, EWS 56120 heads the short trip working, the 6D34 11.16 Healey Mills–Cobra Railfreight 'Enterprise' service at Horbury on 30 July 1999.

West Yorkshire – 'Le Grand Départ'

The sight of a class 47 rolling into Huddersfield station beneath the splendid L&NWR 1880-built overall roof on Saturday 5 July 2014 evoked memories of happier times on our railways as far as traditional loco-hauled services are concerned. DRS 47841 graces the historic station heading the 1Z82 16.50 Scarborough–Liverpool Lime Street additional service in connection with the 'Le Grand Départ' event. Work is currently underway on Network Rail's 'Northern Hub' project, which will see electrification of the Huddersfield line by 2018.

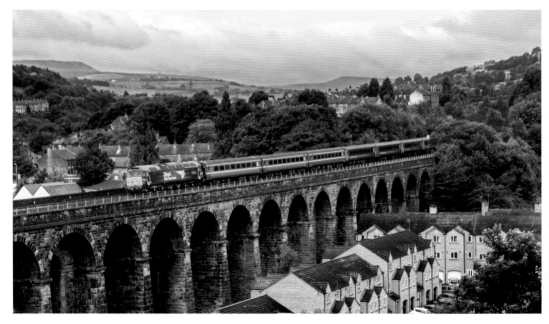

Early morning loco-hauled services over Milnsbridge viaduct (for the sun on this side) are as rare as hen's teeth, but unfortunately the necessary illumination was not to be for this unique opportunity. Ex-works 47810 *Peter Bath MBE*, bearing the new DRS revised 'compass' decals, glides across the viaduct heading the 5Z19 06.12 Crewe Holding Sidings–Leeds empty stock move in connection with additional diagrammed services between Leeds and Harrogate for the 'Le Grand Départ' event on Saturday 5 July 2014.

A rare interlude at Bradford Interchange on Sunday 6 July 2014, with 47810 *Peter Bath MBE* preparing to depart with the 10.21 'Tour de France' special service to Blackburn, and the arrival from Hebden Bridge (going on to Leeds) with DB Schenker 67027 attached to the rear.

Some thought by DRS had gone into presenting 57308 *County of Staffordshire* for the 'Tour de France' services, photographed at Bradford Interchange on Sunday 6 July 2014, but despite the effort there's not a lot that can be done to improve the front end of this former Virgin 'Thunderbird' locomotive. Its previous incarnation as a class 47 before rebuild was 47846 in FGW green livery with gold band and, the more senior reader may recall, D1677 *Thor* allocated to Bristol Bath Road in the 1960s, arguably far more aesthetically pleasing appearances.

No. 47810 *Peter Bath MBE* leaves an exhaust trail in its wake as it tackles the unforgiving climb out of Bradford Interchange heading the 10.21 'Tour de France' special service to Blackburn on Sunday 6 July 2014. DB Schenker 67027 waits in the station with the late-running Hebden Bridge–Leeds service.

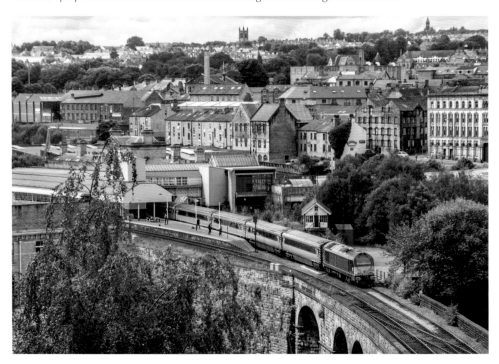

Royal train-liveried Class 67 Skip 67006 *Royal Sovereign* departs Halifax on time heading the 5L03 11.30 Hebden Bridge–Bradford Interchange 'Tour de France' additional service on Sunday 6 July 2014. The class 67 was originally designed for high-speed Royal Mail trains, but within three years of the class being introduced Royal Mail announced it would cease using the forty-nine daily mail trains. After the shock announcement, the EWS fleet of thirty locomotives gradually found other work, including special charter and Royal Train duties.

The grandiose period features of Halifax station, with parts dating from 1855, and Grand Central's 'Adelante' unit 180112 *James Herriot* seem to harmonise as it rolls into the single-island platform of a once grander station, forming the 1D91 11.50 King's Cross–Bradford Interchange via Wakefield Kirkgate on a busy Sunday 6 July 2014 during the 'Tour de France' weekend.

On Sunday 6 July 2014 and running ten minutes late, the 13.05 Bradford Interchange–Blackburn 'Tour de France' additional service glides across Beacon Hill viaduct, passing the historic Bailey Hall Mill, adjacent to the railway station.

The York–Doncaster–Humberside Triangle

'Transrail'-branded 37897 heads the Immingham–Doncaster 'Enterprise' past Barnetby East signal box on 21 July 1999. Delivered from the Vulcan Foundry in July 1963 as D6855 to Landore depot, it was subsequently initially renumbered 37155 under the TOPS scheme and in 1986 as 37897. Placed into storage during March 2000 and subsequently purchased by HNRC, it was finally disposed of at EMR Kingsbury during February 2008.

EWS Romanian Grid 56018 at Hatfield and Stainforth heading the 6D88 Goole–Scunthorpe steel via Belmont yard on 26 August 1999. No. 56018 was subsequently sold to UK Rail Leasing and in July 2014 was at Wabtec's Brush Traction works, expected to be their first Class 56 locomotive available for hire.

Right: Whether you look east or west along the line at Barnetby, the mechanical signalling infrastructure is a joy to behold, exemplified in this view of Transrail-brand 56056 passing Barnetby East signal box with coal from Immingham Dock for Scunthorpe Steelworks on 13 October 2001.

Below: Nos 37252 and 37221 head an Up block petroleum train at Bridge Junction, Doncaster, on 28 July 1978. How this classic view changed with the electrification of the ECML! (Author's Collection)

With heavy rain falling to the south, the low evening sun just highlights Virgin Class 47/8 47828 as it passes Colton South Junction on 13 July 1999 heading to York with two Porterbrook barrier coaches. The Brush Type 4/Class 47s were arguably the most versatile British-built locomotives ever supplied to a railway in Britain, working all manner of freight and passenger services and demonstrating their versatility; the locomotive still remains in service during 2014, with DRS.

Preserved Peak Class 46 D172 *Ixion* (previously 46035) heads the 'Lancastrian' empty charter stock to York, and is seen at Bolton Percy near York shortly before sunset on 27 August 1999. The locomotive is now stored out of use at the 'Railway Age' in Crewe.

When Gascoigne Wood was producing coal, class 58s had a regular turn into North Yorkshire away from their main areas of operation in the Midlands. No. 58002 *Daw Mill Colliery* heads the 7Z32 Milford West Sidings–Ironbridge power station via Toton with thirty-two MGR wagons in tow at South Milford Junction on 13 June 1994. Subsequently receiving the 'Mainline' sector livery and allocated to Eastleigh, 58002 was disposed of by EMR Southampton at the end of 2013.

With Ferrybridge power station looming behind, National Power's 59202 *Vale of White Horse* heads a loaded Gascoigne Wood–Drax service at Knottingley West Junction on 10 September 1997. National Power took delivery of six class 59/2s in 1994–95 from General Motors in Ontario, and their distinctive livery and matching wagons made a striking sight during their short period in this guise.

EWS 56103 *Stora* rounds the curve, powering away from Gascoigne Wood loading point with loaded MGR wagons on 13 March 2001. Happily this Grid is still with us today and has made a main-line comeback in 2014 with Devon & Cornwall Railways.

Built just two years previously, National Power 59203 *Vale of Pickering* returns empties to Gascoigne Wood Colliery along the Eggborough power station branch line on 23 July 1997. The class of six 59/2s were built by GM in Canada for block coal operations in Yorkshire, and were based at Ferrybridge.

National Power 59201 *Vale of York* working to Ferrybridge power station through Castleford on 23 July 1997. Work is underway on the platform for the resignalling work, and the signal box and semaphore signalling were decommissioned on 13 September 1997.

Former Healey Mills stalwart Loadhaul 56021, at Milford Junction, with a train of duff from Gascoigne Wood for Prince of Wales, Pontefract, on 10 September 1997. The Romanian-built Grid was withdrawn from service less than two years later, in June 1999, while still wearing the Loadhaul colour scheme, arguably the most inspired livery of its time and to some degree perpetuated by Colas Railfreight today. It survived in storage for a further decade, latterly at the Long Marston secure store, but was finally cut up in August 2009.

National Power 59205 heads a Drax power station–Gascoigne Wood loading point empty MGR at Whitley Bridge Junction on 10 September 1997.

Transrail Dutch-liveried 56049 heading Scunthorpe–Redcar sinter empties at Brumber Hill, near Colton Junction, on 16 July 1999. After a period of store at Bristol Barton Hill, the Grid was sold on to EMR Kingsbury for scrap in December 2011.

RES-liveried 47737 *Resurgent* heads the 1V64 14.06 Low Fell–Plymouth mail at Bolton Percy, south of York, on 9 July 1999. No. 47769 *Resolve* on the rear of the train would take this train forward upon reversal at Doncaster RMT.

DRS 47853 *Rail Express*, with yellow-painted buffers for the occasion, thunders through the delightful Garforth station in charge of the 06.00 Liverpool Lime Street–York 'Tour de France' additional service on Sunday 6 July 2014. Sadly the fine NER footbridge will soon be removed to make way for the overhead electrification of the route between Leeds and Colton Junction.

Peak 46039, with steam heating boiler working overtime, stands at the head of the 18.51 'Cleveland Executive' departure from York on 25 November 1981. No. 46039 was withdrawn from service in October 1983 and eventually scrapped at BREL Swindon during June 1985.

No. 45107 had just arrived at York with a terminating Trans-Pennine service from Liverpool Lime Street on 26 November 1981. Latterly bearing the unofficial name *Phoenix* and with white window and side grille embellishments, 45107 would remain in service until the end of July 1988, just one week short of the withdrawal of the final members of the class in regular service.

A fleeting glimpse of the perfectly timed low evening sunlight showcases Virgin Class 47/8 No. 47827 heading the 1V67 18.05 Newcastle–Bristol Temple Meads service at Brumber Hill, near Colton South Junction, on 13 July 1999. Delivered new to Bristol Bath Road depot in January 1966 as D1928, it would survive to become one of the class 47s selected to be converted to class 57/3s, emerging from Brush Loughborough in July 2002 as General Motors diesel-powered Thunderbird 57302 *Virgil Tracy*. Subsequently purchased from Virgin Trains by DRS, it now bears their Compass livery and is named *Chad Varah*.

Only three of the fifteen Class 86 locos taken over by EWS were repainted in the company's red and gold livery. No. 86261 *The Rail Charter Partnership* heads the Low Fell–Bristol mail at Bolton Percy on 16 August 1999. Originally delivered new from BR Doncaster works in October 1965 as E3118, it was withdrawn from service in November 2002 and scrapped during December 2004 at Booth Roe's Rotherham scrapyard.

On 25 November 1981, with just over a month remaining in service, the sound of the twin Napier Deltic engines of 55021 *Argyll & Sutherland Highlander* would soon fall silent. As she was waiting in the Up bay platforms at York waiting to depart for King's Cross, the noise was incredibly moving – 'music to the ear', with the platform vibrating. This locomotive hauled the final King's Cross–York Deltic-hauled service on 31 December 1981, the 1L41 09.40 King's Cross–York.

The fumes linger beneath the magnificent overall station roof at York as 47414, heading the 00.02 King's Cross–Newcastle, waits for the road on 26 July 1980. This class 47 was one of the original East Coast members displacing steam traction, being delivered new to Finsbury Park (34G) depot in March 1963 as D1513. An Eastern Region-allocated loco throughout its service, it was withdrawn from Gateshead depot in March 1986 and disposed of by Vic Berry, Leicester, in May 1989.

Class 40 No. 40086 of York depot heads a Scarborough summer-dated service, with the loco about to run round as adjacent Class 45/0 Peak No. 45006 *Honourable Artillery Company* of Tinsley depot heads the 13.40 Newcastle–Swansea at York on Saturday 26 July 1980. Built by English Electric at their Vulcan works (W/No. E2808/D523) as D286, it entered service in July 1960 and was allocated to Gateshead depot. It remained in the 'east' throughout its career, spending its time at Neville Hill, York and Gateshead depots, from where it was finally withdrawn in January 1985 and cut up at BR Doncaster works during the following month. No. 45006 was introduced to service from BR Crewe works in March 1961 as D89 and was withdrawn in September 1986 and scrapped at Vic Berry's scrapyard in Leicester during October 1988.

Loadhaul-branded 60007 (formerly named *Robert Adam*) heading the 6D43 14.05 Jarrow–Lindsey empty petroleum bogie tankers at Otterington, north of Thirsk, on Monday 13 September 1999. The locomotive now bears the striking DB Schenker red livery as a 'Super Tug' and carries the name *The Spirit of Tom Kendell*, in memory of a DB Schenker worker killed in a road accident.

Deltic No. 55013 *The Black Watch* at the head of the 08.07 departure from York to London King's Cross on a damp 26 November 1981. Withdrawn just a few weeks later in December 1981, this class 55 was one of the many that never made it into preservation, meeting its fate at Doncaster works one year later.

The English Electric prototype Co-Co DP2 approaching York at Holgate heading the 1A18 from King's Cross in August 1963. It was introduced into service in February 1962 and had a sixteen-cylinder 2,700 hp engine in a body based on that of the production Deltics. Its electronic control systems were later modified to enable it to become the forerunner of the class 50. In July 1967 it was involved in a serious accident at Thirsk when it collided at speed with a derailed cement train. It was withdrawn from service in September and was returned to the manufacturer for component recovery and eventual scrap. (the late Colin Whitfield/www.railphotoprints.co.uk)

The end of the 1986/87 winter timetable saw the loss of the Class 45/1 passenger turns on the Trans-Pennine route; however, the summer of 1987 did find a number of diagrams operated by class 45/1s deputising the class 47/4s. There were also a number of summer-dated diagrams that returned the class to passenger haulage, in between their regular duties in charge of newspaper, mail and van trains. On 3 June 1987, 45103 was in charge of a North Trans-Pennine service at York. By August 1988, 45103 was one of only four active non-departmental class 45s left in service, and after a career spanning almost twenty-seven years was withdrawn (along with the other three: 45046, 45128 and 45141) when regular operation of the Peaks ended. It was subsequently stored at Tinsley TMD until March 1990 when, along with 45107, 45110, 45113 and 45115, it was towed from Tinsley to MC Metals at Glasgow and was broken up shortly after arrival.

Ex-works 50027 *Lion* working the 09.50 Edinburgh–Plymouth through Selby on 28 July 1983. The outshopped class 50s from Doncaster were generally returned to the Western Region by this diagram. The class 50s were the last mixed-traffic class to be built by BR. (Graham Roose)

Deltic 55016 *Gordon Highlander* heads an Up service for London King's Cross through Selby station on 30 May 1978. Withdrawn in December 1981, the Deltic survived the cutter's torch and was purchased privately, initially as a source of spares for sister loco 55022 *Royal Scots Grey*. It is the intention, subject to funding, to restore it to full main-line condition for operation on Network Rail. (Graham Roose)

Grimsby Town station on 27 July 1980, with the pilot loco, 08478 of Immingham depot, stabled between duties.

Leaving a trail of dust in their wake, 37683 and 37688 pass the former station at Melton heading the Rylstone–Hull Tilcon limestone on 13 April 1992.

On 27 July 1980 infrastructure from the steam age abounds as 08567 stands in the yard at Goole Docks, the most inland port on the east coast, some 50 miles along the Humber River from the North Sea. The shunter, originally delivered in April 1959 as D3734 to Edinburgh St Margaret's depot, was still extant in August 2014, bearing the EWS maroon and gold livery, although it was in store at Crewe International T&RSMD.

DRS 37218 stands at Hull King George Dock on 9 November 2004, having just arrived with containerised uranium from Sellafield for export to Russia. No. 37218 is still active with DRS and now bears the company's revised Compass branding introduced during 2014.

Autumn colours abound as EWS 66012 and 66156 top and tail a Grimsby–Doncaster Railhead Treatment train at Barnetby East on 9 November 2009.

No. 60084 *Cross Fell* at Melton Ross heading the 6T24 11.33 Immingham Docks–Santon iron ore on 2 October 1999.

EWS 56068 heads the Roxby Gullet–Northenden empty Binliner containerised waste through Hatfield and Stainforth on 2 September 1999.

Dutch-liveried 56031 heading a Goole–Doncaster 'Enterprise' service, comprising ISO container wagons and two 'pig pen' sliding-hood steel-coil wagons, passing Hatfield and Stainforth on 21 September 1999. The leading unladen and recently built 'FAA' swan-neck container wagon has a massive tare weight of 33.5 tonnes, but offers the sought-after high cube (9-foot-6-inch-high ISO containers) gauge capability over the routes serving the East Coast ports. No. 56031 was the first of the BREL Doncaster-built class 56s introduced into service in May 1977. Named *Merehead* in September 1983, by the time of this photograph it had lost its nameplates. It was one of a number of the class hired by Fertis for use in France and Spain on construction and maintenance trains. Following repatriation it was sold to EMR Kingsbury in January 2013 for scrap, but in summer 2014 could be found at the former Leicester depot site and miraculously may be restored to main-line condition once more.

EWS 60055 *Thomas Barnardo*, bearing Transrail decals, heads the Northenden–Roxby Gullet household waste Binliner train past Hatfield Colliery, Stainforth, on 4 August 1999. This is the site of the colliery spoil heap landslide that occurred in February 2013, with the resultant closure of the route for many weeks.

Resplendent in its British Steel blue livery, 60006 *Scunthorpe Steelmaster* heads the 6D73 14.56 Lindsey Oil Refinery–Leeds Hunslet East ORT at Knabb's Crossing, Melton Ross, on 6 September 1999. No. 60006 was later to receive the Corus corporate silver livery.

Nos 37106 and 37351 work an afternoon Immingham Dock–Santon ore terminal through Elsham station in August 1989. (Adrian Freeman)

Doncaster in the early hours of 26 July 1980, with 31202 waiting with an Up parcels service. Introduced into BR service as D5626 in June 1960, this loco suffered an ignominious fate and was one of two that ran away at Cricklewood depot. The incident was on 28 October 1988 and involved 31202 and 31226. No. 31202 was the leading loco and was withdrawn immediately, being cut into two halves on site at Cricklewood prior to removal by road to Vic Berry's scrapyard in Leicester for disposal.

Class 55 Deltic 55002 *The King's Own Yorkshire Light Infantry* has just arrived at Doncaster station at 01.05 on Friday 26 July 1980, having brought in the 1D26 (FO) 23.40 Hull–Paignton. The throbbing Deltic has just detached from the stock to allow a Class 46, No. 46016, to take the service forward as the late-running 00.57 departure to Paignton.

Class 40 No. 40006 whistles away the time at Platform 15 at York at the head of a Saturday extra service from Llandudno to York on a wet 14 June 1980. Built by English Electric at their Vulcan Foundry, it entered BR service as D206 in July 1958. Withdrawn in March 1983, the veteran BR 'Early Modernisation Plan' Type 4 was cut up at Crewe works during August 1984.

Having just arrived from Edinburgh, Class 55 Deltic 55019 *Royal Highland Fusilier* removes a parcels vehicle from the head of its train and shunts it into one of the Up bay platforms before moving back on to its service train, the 01.05 departure from York to King's Cross. Station pilot 08525 on the adjacent line patiently awaits further instructions. This was 26 November 1981, and in just four weeks 55019 was to be withdrawn from service. This locomotive hauled the final Deltic-hauled BR service train, the 16.30 Aberdeen–York on 31 December 1981.

No. 55007 *Pinza*, in its Finsbury Park special livery with white window surrounds, heads light engine to York depot, having arrived with the 14.05 service from King's Cross on 14 June 1980. It would later return to the capital in charge of the 19.55 departure from York.

Having just taken on water from the hydrant seen on the left, Class 55 Deltic No. 55004 *Queen's Own Highlander* prepares to depart from York heading the 22.30 King's Cross–Edinburgh service on 26 July 1980. As Platform 14 vibrated and the twin Napier Deltic engines added their melody to the still of the night, the author had this most memorable occasion to himself; there were no other observers around in the wee small hours, quite understandably! No. 55004 was to remain in service for just over one more year, being withdrawn in November 1981 and finally cut up at Doncaster works in August 1983.